CW01221258

JARROLD POETS SERIES

Also in this series:

Robert and Elizabeth Browning
Robert Burns
Lord Byron
Samuel Taylor Coleridge
John Keats
Rudyard Kipling
The Lady Poets
Scottish Poems & Ballads
Percy Bysshe Shelley
Alfred, Lord Tennyson
The War Poets
William Wordsworth
Animal Poems
Childhood Poems
Love Poems
Patriotic Poems
Sea Poems

PASTORAL POEMS - AN ANTHOLOGY

Poems selected by Ron Hawkins
Designed by Parke Sutton Publishing Limited
for Jarrold Publishing, Norwich
First published 1994

ISBN 0-7117-0680-8

CONTENTS

HENRY HOWARD, EARL OF SURREY (?1517–47)
Spring 9
THOMAS SACKVILLE, EARL OF DORSET (1536–1608)
Winter 10
EDMUND SPENSER (?1552–99)
From: Prothalamion 11
MICHAEL DRAYTON (1563–1631)
Clear Had the Day 16
CHRISTOPHER MARLOWE (1564–93)
The Passionate Shepherd to his Love 17
The Argument of His Book 19
WILLIAM SHAKESPEARE (1564–1616)
Sonnets: How Like a Winter Hath my Absence Been 20
   From You Have I Been Absent in the Spring 21
THOMAS NASHE (1567–1601)
Spring, the Sweet Spring 22
ROBERT HERRICK (1591–1674)
To Meadows 23
To Daffodils 24
JOHN MILTON (1608–74)
From: Paradise Lost 25

On May Morning	26
RICHARD LOVELACE (1618–57)	
The Grasshopper	27
ABRAHAM COWLEY (1618–67)	
From: Of Solitude	29
ANDREW MARVELL (1621–78)	
The Garden	30
ANNE, COUNTESS OF WINCHILSEA (?1660–1720)	
A Nocturnal Reverie	34
ALEXANDER POPE (1688–1744)	
From: Windsor Forest	37
Solitude.	38
JAMES THOMSON (1700–48)	
From: The Seasons	39
THOMAS GRAY (1716–71)	
From: Elegy Written in a Country Churchyard . . .	43
OLIVER GOLDSMITH (1728–74)	
From: The Deserted Village.	49
WILLIAM COWPER (1731–1800)	
From: The Task	52
The Stream	54

ANNA LETITIA BARBAULD (1743–1825)
Ode to Spring 55
GEORGE CRABBE (1754–1832)
Birds in Winter 58
WILLIAM BLAKE (1757–1827)
The Shepherd 59
JOANNA BAILLIE (1762–1851)
From: Hay Making 60
WILLIAM WORDSWORTH (1770–1850)
From: Lines Composed a Few Miles above
   Tintern Abbey 62
The Solitary Reaper 68
The Daffodils 70
SAMUEL TAYLOR COLERIDGE (1772–1834)
To Nature 72
EBENEZER ELLIOTT (1741–1849)
Spring 73
PERCY BYSSHE SHELLEY (1792–1822)
Summer and Winter 74
Ode to the West Wind 75

JOHN CLARE (1793–1866)

The Shepherd's Tree 80

Autumn 81

JOHN KEATS (1795–1821)

To Autumn 82

From: Endymion 84

THOMAS HOOD (1799–1845)

From: Autumn 86

ELIZABETH BARRETT BROWNING (1806–61)

From: Aurora Leigh 88

ALFRED, LORD TENNYSON (1809–92)

From: In Memoriam 91

ROBERT BROWNING (1812–89)

The Year's at the Spring 95

Home Thoughts, from Abroad 95

DANTE GABRIEL ROSSETTI (1828–82)

Silent Noon 97

GEORGE MEREDITH (1828–1909)

We Saw the Swallows 98

CHRISTINA ROSSETTI (1830–94)

Spring Quiet 99

THOMAS HARDY (1840–1928)
Afterwards *101*
GERARD MANLEY HOPKINS (1844–89)
The Windhover *103*
Pied Beauty *105*
Spring *106*
ROBERT BRIDGES (1844–1930)
From: November *107*
A.E. HOUSMAN (1859–1936)
From: A Shropshire Lad *109*
Loveliest of Trees, the Cherry Now . . . *111*
RUDYARD KIPLING (1865–1936)
The Way Through the Woods *112*
From: A Charm *113*
W.B. YEATS (1865–1939)
The Lake Isle of Innisfree *114*
The Wild Swans at Coole *115*
CHARLOTTE MEW (1869–1928)
In the Fields *117*
The Trees are Down *118*

Laurence Binyon (1869–1943)
From: The Burning of the Leaves 121
William H. Davies (1870–1940)
Leisure 123
Born of Tears 124
Edward Thomas (1878–1917)
Sedge-warblers 125
Thaw 126
There's Nothing Like the Sun 127
John Drinkwater (1882–1937)
Sonnet 128

Henry Howard, Earl of Surrey

Spring

The sweet season, that bud and bloom forth brings,
With green hath clad the hill and eke the vale;
The nightingale with feathers new she sings,
The turtle to her mate hath told her tale.
Summer is come, for every spray now springs,
The hart hath hung his old head on the pale,
The buck in brake his winter coat he flings,
The fishes float the new-repairèd scale:
The adder all her slough away she slings,
The swift swallow pursueth the flies small,
The busy bee her honey now she mings;
Winter is worn that was the flowers' bale:
   And thus I see, among these pleasant things
   Each care decays, – and yet my sorrow springs.

Thomas Sackville, Earl of Dorset

Winter

The wrathful winter, 'proaching on apace,
  With blustering blasts had all ybared the treen,
And old Saturnus, with his frosty face,
  With chilling cold had pierced the tender green,
The mantles rent, wherein enwrappèd been
    The gladsome groves that now lay over-thrown,
    The tapets torn, and every bloom down blown.

And sorrowing I to see the summer flowers,
  The lively green, the lusty leas forlorn,
The sturdy trees so shattered with the showers,
  The fields so fade that flourished so beforn,
It taught me well all earthly things be born
    To die the death, for naught long time may last:
    The summer's beauty yields to winter's blast.

Edmund Spenser

From: Prothalamion

Calm was the day, and through the trembling air
Sweet-breathing Zephyrus did softly play,
A gentle spirit, that lightly did delay
Hot Titan's beams, which then did glister fair;
When I (whom sullen care,
Through discontent of my long fruitless stay
In princes' court, and expectation vain
Of idle hopes, which still do fly away
Like empty shadows, did afflict my brain)
Walked forth to ease my pain
Along the shore of silver-streaming Thames;
Whose rutty bank, the which his river hems,
Was painted all with variable flowers,
And all the meads adorned with dainty gems
Fit to deck maidens' bowers,
And crown the paramours
Against the bridal day, which is not long:
    Sweet Thames, run softly, till I end my song.

There in a meadow by the river's side
A flock of nymphs I chancèd to espy,
All lovely daughters of the flood thereby,
With goodly greenish locks all loose untied,
As each had been a bride;
And each one had a little wicker basket
Made of fine twigs, entrailèd curiously,
In which they gathered flowers to fill their flasket,
And with fine fingers cropt full feateously
The tender stalks on high.
Of every sort which in that meadow grew
They gathered some; the violet, pallid blue,
The little daisy that at evening closes,
The virgin lily and the primrose true,
With store of vermeil roses,
To deck their bridegrooms' posies
Against the bridal day, which was not long:
    Sweet Thames, run softly, till I end my song.

With that, I saw two swans of goodly hue
Come softly swimming down along the lee;
Two fairer birds I yet did never see;
The snow which doth the top of Pindus strew
Did never whiter shew,

*Nor Jove himself, when he a swan would be
For love of Leda, whiter did appear;
Yet Leda was, they say, as white as he,
Yet not so white as these, nor nothing near;
So purely white they were,
That even the gentle stream, the which them bare,
Seemed foul to them, and bade his billows spare
To wet their silken feathers, lest they might
Soil their fair plumes with water not so fair,
And mar their beauties bright,
That shone as heaven's light
Against their bridal day, which was not long:*
    Sweet Thames, run softly, till I end my song.

*Eftsoons the nymphs, which now had flowers their fill,
Ran all in haste to see that silver brood,
As they came floating on the crystal flood;
Whom when they saw, they stood amazèd still,
Their wondering eyes to fill,
Them seemed they never saw a sight so fair
Of fowls so lovely, that they sure did deem
Them heavenly born, or to be that same pair
Which through the sky draw Venus' silver team;
For sure they did not seem*

To be begot of any earthly seed,
But rather angels, or of angels' breed;
Yet were they bred of Somers-heat, they say,
In sweetest season, when each flower and weed
The earth did fresh array;
So fresh they seemed as day,
Even as their bridal day, which was not long:
   Sweet Thames, run softly, till I end my song.

Then forth they all out of their baskets drew
Great store of flowers, the honour of the field,
That to the sense did fragrant odours yield,
All which upon those goodly birds they threw,
And all the waves did strew,
That like old Peneus' waters they did seem,
When down along by pleasant Tempe's shore,
Scattered with flowers, through Thessaly they stream,
That they appear, through lilies' plenteous store,
Like a bride's chamber-floor.
Two of those nymphs meanwhile two garlands bound
Of freshest flowers which in that mead they found,
The which presenting all in trim array,
Their snowy foreheads therewithal they crowned,
Whilst one did sing this lay

Prepared against that day,
Against their bridal day, which was not long:
   Sweet Thames, run softly, till I end my song.

"*Ye gentle birds, the world's fair ornament,*
And heaven's glory, whom this happy hour
Doth lead unto your lovers' blissful bower,
Joy may you have and gentle heart's content
Of your love's couplement;
And let fair Venus, that is queen of love,
With her heart-quelling son upon you smile,
Whose smile, they say, hath virtue to remove
All love's dislike, and friendship's faulty guile
For ever to assoil.
Let endless peace your steadfast hearts accord,
And blessed plenty wait upon your board;
And let your bed with pleasures chaste abound,
That fruitful issue may to you afford,
Which may your foes confound,
And make your joys redound,
Upon your bridal day, which is not long:
   Sweet Thames, run softly, till I end my song."

Michael Drayton

Clear Had the Day ...

Clear had the day been from the dawn,
All chequered was the sky,
Thin clouds like scarfs of cobweb lawn
Veiled heaven's most glorious eye.

The wind had no more strength than this,
That leisurely it blew
To make one leaf the next to kiss
That closely by it grew.

The rills that on the pebbles played
Might now be heard at will;
This world they only music made,
Else everything was still.

Christopher Marlowe

The Passionate Shepherd to his Love

Come live with me and be my love,
And we will all the pleasures prove
That hills and valleys, dale and field,
And all the craggy mountains yield.

There will we sit upon the rocks
And see the shepherds feed their flocks,
By shallow rivers, to whose falls
Melodious birds sing madrigals.

There will I make thee beds of roses
And a thousand fragrant posies,
A cap of flowers, and a kirtle
Embroidered all with leaves of myrtle;

A gown made of the finest wool,
Which from our pretty lambs we pull,
Fair linèd slippers for the cold,
With buckles of the purest gold.

A belt of straw and ivy buds,
With coral clasps and amber studs:
And if these pleasures may thee move,
Come live with me and be my love.

The shepherd swains shall dance and sing
For thy delight each May-morning:
If these delights thy mind may move,
Then live with me and be my love.

Christopher Marlowe

The Argument of His Book

*I sing of brooks, of blossoms, birds and bowers,
Of April, May, of June and July-flowers;
I sing of May-poles, hock-carts, wassails, wakes,
Of bridegrooms, brides and of their bridal cakes;
I write of youth, of love, and have access
By these to sing of cleanly wantonness;
I sing of dews, of rains, and piece by piece
Of balm, of oil, of spice and ambergris;
I sing of times trans-shifting, and I write
How roses first came red and lilies white;
I write of groves, of twilights, and I sing
The Court of Mab, and of the Fairy King;
I write of hell; I sing (and ever shall)
Of heaven, and hope to have it after all.*

William Shakespeare

Sonnet XCVII

How like a winter hath my absence been
From thee, the pleasure of the fleeting year!
What freezings have I felt, what dark days seen!
What old December's bareness every where!
And yet this time remov'd was summer's time;
The teeming autumn, big with rich increase,
Bearing the wanton burden of the prime,
Like widow'd wombs after their lords' decease:
Yet this abundant issue seem'd to me
But hope of orphans and unfather'd fruit;
For summer and his pleasures wait on thee,
And, thou away, the very birds are mute:
    Or, if they sing, 'tis with so dull a cheer,
    That leaves look pale, dreading the winter's near.

William Shakespeare

Sonnet XCVIII

From you have I been absent in the spring,
When proud-pied April, dress'd in all his trim,
Hath put a spirit of youth in every thing,
That heavy Saturn laugh'd and leap'd with him.
Yet nor the lays of birds, nor the sweet smell
Of different flowers in odour and in hue,
Could make me any summer's story tell,
Or from their proud lap pluck them where they grew:
Nor did I wonder at the lily's white,
Nor praise the deep vermilion in the rose;
They were but sweet, but figures of delight,
Drawn after you, you pattern of all those.
   Yet seem'd it winter still, and, you away,
   As with your shadow I with these did play.

Thomas Nashe

Spring, the Sweet Spring

Spring, the sweet spring, is the year's pleasant king;
Then blooms each thing, then maids dance in a ring,
Cold doth not sting, the pretty birds do sing:
   Cuckoo, jug-jug, pu-we, to-witta-woo!

The palm and may make country houses gay,
Lambs frisk and play, the shepherds pipe all day,
And we hear aye birds tune this merry lay:
   Cuckoo, jug-jug, pu-we, to-witta-woo!

The fields breathe sweet, the daisies kiss our feet,
Young lovers meet, old wives a-sunning sit,
In every street these tunes our ears do greet:
   Cuckoo, jug-jug, pu-we, to-witta-woo!
     Spring, the sweet spring!

Robert Herrick

To Meadows

Ye have been fresh and green,
Ye have been filled with flowers:
And ye the walks have been
Where maids have spent their hours.

You have beheld, how they
With wicker arks did come
To kiss, and bear away
The richer cowslips home.

Ye have heard them sweetly sing,
And seen them in a round:
Each virgin, like a spring,
With honey-suckles crowned.

But now we see none here,
Whose silvery feet did tread,
And with dishevelled hair,
Adorned this smoother mead.

Like unthrifts, having spent
Your stock and needy grown,
Ye are left here to lament
Your poor estates, alone.

Robert Herrick

To Daffodils

Fair Daffodils, we weep to see
  You haste away so soon:
As yet the early-rising sun
  Has not attained his noon.
    Stay, stay,
  Until the hasting day
    Has run
  But to the even-song;
And, having prayed together, we
  Will go with you along.

We have short time to stay as you,
  We have as short a spring;
As quick a growth to meet decay
  As you, or any thing,
    We die
  As your hours do, and dry
    Away
  Like to the summer's rain;
Or as the pearls of morning's dew,
  Ne'er to be found again.

John Milton

From: Paradise Lost

*So on he fares, and to the border comes
Of Eden, where delicious Paradise,
Now nearer, crowns with her enclosure green
As with a rural mound the champaign head
Of a steep wilderness, whose hairy sides
With thicket overgrown, grotesque and wild,
Access denied; and overhead up grew
Insuperable highth of loftiest shade,
Cedar, and pine, and fir, and branching palm,
A sylvan scene, and as the ranks ascend
Shade above shade, a woody theater
Of stateliest view. Yet higher than their tops
The verdurous wall of Paradise up sprung;
Which to our general sire gave prospect large
Into his nether empire neighboring round.
And higher than that wall a circling row
Of goodliest trees loaden with fairest fruit,
Blossoms and fruits at once of golden hue,
Appeared, with gay enameled colors mixed;
On which the sun more glad impressed his beams*

Than in fair evening cloud, or humid bow,
When God hath show'red the earth; so lovely seemed
That landscape.

ON MAY MORNING

Now the bright morning-star, day's harbinger,
Comes dancing from the east, and leads with her
The flowery May, who from her green lap throws
The yellow cowslip and the pale primrose.
   Hail, bounteous May, that dost inspire
   Mirth and youth and warm desire;
     Woods and groves are of thy dressing,
     Hill and dale doth boast thy blessing.
Thus we salute thee with our early song,
And welcome thee, and wish thee long.

Richard Lovelace

The Grasshopper

O thou that swing'st upon the waving ear
Of some well-fillèd oaten beard,
Drunk every night with a delicious tear
Dropped thee from Heaven, where now th'art reared,

The joys of earth and air are thine entire,
That with thy feet and wings dost hop and fly;
And, when thy poppy works, thou dost retire
To thy carved acorn-bed to lie.

Up with the day, the sun thou welcom'st then,
Sport'st in the gilt-plats of his beams,
And all these merry days mak'st merry men,
Thyself, and melancholy streams.

But ah the sickle! golden ears are cropt:
Ceres and Bacchus bid goodnight;
Sharp frosty fingers all your flowers have topt,
And what scythes spared, winds shave off quite.

Poor verdant fool! and now green ice! thy joys,
Large and as lasting as thy perch of grass,

Bid us lay in 'gainst winter rain, and poise
Their floods, with an o'erflowing glass.

Thou best of men and friends! we will create
A genuine summer in each other's breast;
And spite of this cold time and frozen fate
Thaw us a warm seat to our rest.

Our sacred hearths shall burn eternally
As vestal flames; the north-wind, he
Shall strike his frost-stretched wings, dissolve and fly
This Ætna in epitome.

Dropping December shall come weeping in,
Bewail th'usurping of his reign;
But when in show'rs of old Greek we begin,
Shall cry, he hath his crown again!

Night as clear Hesper shall our tapers whip
From the light casements where we play,
And the dark hag from her black mantle strip,
And stick there, everlasting Day.

Thus richer than untempted kings are we,
That asking nothing, nothing need:
Though lord of all that seas embrace, yet he
That wants himself, is poor indeed.

Abraham Cowley

From: Of Solitude

Hail, old patrician trees, so great and good!
　Hail, ye plebeian underwood!
　　Where the poetic birds rejoice,
And for their quiet nests and plenteous food,
　Pay with their grateful voice.

* * *

Here Nature does a house for me erect,
　Nature the wisest architect,
　　Who those fond artists does despise
That can the fair and living trees neglect,
　Yet the dead timber prize.

Here let me, careless and unthoughtful lying,
　Hear the soft winds, above me flying,
　　With all their wanton boughs dispute,
And the more tuneful birds to both replying,
　Nor be myself too mute.

Andrew Marvell

The Garden

How vainly men themselves amaze
To win the palm, the oak, or bays,
And their uncessant labours see
Crowned from some single herb or tree,
Whose short and narrow-vergèd shade
Does prudently their toils upbraid;
While all the flowers and trees do close
To weave the garlands of repose.

Fair Quiet, have I found thee here,
And Innocence thy sister dear!
Mistaken long, I sought you then
In busy companies of men.
Your sacred plants, if here below,
Only among the plants will grow:
Society is all but rude,
To this delicious solitude.

No white nor red was ever seen
So amorous as this lovely green.

Fond lovers, cruel as their flame,
Cut in these trees their mistress' name:
Little, alas, they know or heed
How far these beauties hers exceed!
Fair trees! wheresoe'er your barks I wound,
No name shall but your own be found.

When we have run our passions' heat
Love hither makes his best retreat.
The gods, that mortal beauty chase,
Still in a tree did end their race:
Apollo hunted Daphne so,
Only that she might laurel grow;
And Pan did after Syrinx speed,
Not as a nymph, but for a reed.

What wondrous life in this I lead!
Ripe apples drop about my head;
The luscious clusters of the vine
Upon my mouth do crush their wine;
The nectarine and curious peach
Into my hands themselves do reach;
Stumbling on melons, as I pass,
Ensnared with flowers, I fall on grass.

Meanwhile the mind, from pleasure less,
Withdraws into its happiness;
The mind, that ocean where each kind
Does straight its own resemblance find;
Yet it creates, transcending these,
Far other worlds, and other seas;
Annihilating all that's made
To a green thought in a green shade.

Here at the fountain's sliding foot
Or at some fruit-tree's mossy root,
Casting the body's vest aside,
My soul into the boughs does glide:
There like a bird it sits and sings,
Then whets and combs its silver wings,
And, till prepared for longer flight,
Waves in its plumes the various light.

Such was that happy garden-state
While man there walked without a mate:
After a place so pure and sweet,
What other help could yet be meet!
But 'twas beyond a mortal's share
To wander solitary there:
Two paradises 'twere in one,
To live in Paradise alone.

How well the skilful gardener drew
Of flowers and herbs this dial new,
Where, from above, the milder sun
Does through a fragrant zodiac run:
And, as it works, th' industrious bee
Computes its time as well as we.
How could such sweet and wholesome hours
Be reckoned, but with herbs and flowers?

Anne, Countess of Winchilsea

A Nocturnal Reverie

In such a night, when every louder wind
Is to its distant cavern safe confined;
And only gentle zephyr fans his wings,
And lonely Philomel, still waking, sings;
Or from some tree, famed for the owl's delight,
She, holloaing clear, directs the wanderers right:
In such a night, when passing clouds give place,
Or thinly veil the heaven's mysterious face;
When in some river, overhung with green,
The waving moon and trembling leaves are seen;
When freshened grass now bears itself upright,
And makes cool banks to pleasing rest invite,
Whence springs the woodbind, and the bramble-rose,
And where the sleepy cowslip sheltered grows;
Whilst now a paler hue the foxglove takes,
Yet chequers still with red the dusky brakes:
When scattered glow-worms, but in twilight fine,
Show trivial beauties watch their hour to shine;
Whilst Salisbury stands the test of every light,
In perfect charms and perfect virtue bright.

When odours, which declined repelling day,
Thro' temperate air uninterrupted stray;
When darkened groves their softest shadows wear
And falling waters we distinctly hear;
When through the gloom more venerable shows
Some ancient fabric, awful in repose,
While sunburnt hills their swarthy looks conceal,
And swelling haycocks thicken up the vale:
When the loosed horse now, as his pasture leads,
Comes slowly grazing through the adjoining meads.
Whose stealing pace, and lengthened shade we fear,
Till torn-up forage in his teeth we hear:
When nibbling sheep at large pursue their food,
And unmolested kine re-chew the cud;
When curlews cry beneath the village walls,
And to her straggling brood the partridge calls;
Their short-lived jubilee the creatures keep,
Which but endures, while tyrant man does sleep:
When a sedate content the spirit feels,
And no fierce light disturbs, whilst it reveals;
But silent musings urge the mind to seek
Something, too high for syllables to speak;
Till the free soul to a composedness charmed,
Finding the elements of rage disarmed,

O'er all below a solemn quiet grown,
Joys in the inferior world, and thinks it like her own:
In such a night let me abroad remain,
Till morning breaks, and all's confused again;
Our cares, our toils, our clamours are renewed,
Our pleasures, seldom reached, again pursued.

Alexander Pope

From: Windsor Forest

Thou, too, great father of the British floods!
With joyful pride survey'st our lofty woods;
Where towering oaks their growing honours rear
And future navies on thy shores appear.
Not Neptune's self from all her streams receives
A wealthier tribute, than to thine he gives.
No seas so rich, so gay no banks appear.
No lake so gentle, and no spring so clear.
Nor Po so swells the fabling poet's lays,
While led along the skies his current strays,
As thine, which visits Windsor's famed abodes,
To grace the mansion of our earthly gods:
Nor all his stars above a lustre show,
Like the bright beauties on thy banks below;
Where Jove, subdued by mortal passion still,
Might change Olympus for a nobler hill.

Alexander Pope

Solitude

Happy the man whose wish and care
A few paternal acres bound,
Content to breathe his native air
    In his own ground.

Whose herds with milk, whose fields with bread,
Whose flocks supply him with attire;
Whose trees in summer yield him shade,
    In winter fire.

Blest, who can unconcern'dly find
Hours, days, and years slide soft away
In health of body, peace of mind;
    Quiet by day.

Sound sleep by night; study and ease
Together mixed; sweet recreation;
And innocence, which most does please
    With meditation.

Thus let me live, unseen, unknown;
Thus unlamented let me die;
Steal from the world, and not a stone
    Tell where I lie.

James Thomson

Two pictures from The Seasons

(i)
Snow

The keener tempests come: and, fuming dun
From all the livid east or piercing north,
Thick clouds ascend, in whose capacious womb
A vapoury deluge lies, to snow congealed.
Heavy they roll their fleecy world along,
And the sky saddens with the gathered storm.
Through the hushed air the whitening shower descends,
At first thin-wavering; till at last the flakes
Fall broad and wide and fast, dimming the day
With a continual flow. The cherished fields
Put on their winter-robe of purest white.
'Tis brightness all; save where the new snow melts
Along the mazy current. Low the woods
Bow their hoar head; and, ere the languid sun
Faint from the west emits his evening ray,
Earth's universal face, deep-hid and chill,
Is one wild dazzling waste, that buries wide
The works of man. Drooping, the labourer-ox

Stands covered o'er with snow, and then demands
The fruit of all his toil. The fowls of heaven,
Tamed by the cruel season, crowd around
The winnowing store, and claim the little boon
Which Providence assigns them. One alone,
The redbreast, sacred to the household gods,
Wisely regardful of the embroiling sky,
In joyless fields and thorny thickets leaves
His shivering mates, and pays to trusted man
His annual visit. Half afraid, he first
Against the window beats; then brisk alights
On the warm hearth; then, hopping o'er the floor,
Eyes all the smiling family askance,
And pecks, and starts, and wonders where he is;
Till, more familiar grown, the table-crumbs
Attract his slender feet. The foodless wilds
Pour forth their brown inhabitants. The hare,
Though timorous of heart, and hard beset
By death in various forms, dark snares, and dogs,
And more unpitying men, the garden seeks,
Urged on by fearless want. The bleating kind
Eye the black heaven, and next the glistening earth,
With looks of dumb despair; then, sad dispersed,
Dig for the withered herb through heaps of snow.

(ii)
Frost at Night

With the fierce rage of winter deep suffused,
An icy gale, oft shifting, o'er the pool
Breathes a blue film, and in its mid career
Arrests the bickering stream. The loosened ice,
Let down the flood and half dissolved by day,
Rustles no more; but to the sedgy bank
Fast grows, or gathers round the pointed stone,
A crystal pavement, by the breath of heaven
Cemented firm; till, seized from shore to shore,
The whole imprisoned river growls below.
Loud rings the frozen earth, and hard reflects
A double noise; while, at his evening watch,
The village dog deters the nightly thief;
The heifer lows; the distant water-fall
Swells in the breeze; and with the hasty tread
Of traveller the hollow-sounding plain
Shakes from afar. The full ethereal round,
Infinite worlds disclosing to the view,
Shines out intensely keen; and, all one cope

Of starry glitter, glows from pole to pole.
From pole to pole the rigid influence falls,
Through the still night, incessant, heavy, strong,
And seizes nature fast. It freezes on;
Till morn, late-rising o'er the drooping world,
Lifts her pale eye unjoyous.

Thomas Gray

From: Elegy Written in a Country Churchyard

The curfew tolls the knell of parting day,
The lowing herd wind slowly o'er the lea,
The ploughman homeward plods his weary way,
And leaves the world to darkness and to me.

Now fades the glimmering landscape on the sight,
And all the air a solemn stillness holds,
Save where the beetle wheels his droning flight,
And drowsy tinklings lull the distant folds;

Save that from yonder ivy-mantled tower
The moping owl does to the moon complain
Of such as, wandering near her secret bower,
Molest her ancient solitary reign.

Beneath those rugged elms, that yew-tree's shade,
Where heaves the turf in many a mouldering heap
Each in his narrow cell for ever laid,
The rude forefathers of the hamlet sleep.

The breezy call of incense-breathing morn,
The swallow twittering from the straw-built shed,
The cock's shrill clarion, or the echoing horn,
No more shall rouse them from their lowly bed.

For them no more the blazing hearth shall burn,
Or busy housewife ply her evening care:
No children run to lisp their sire's return,
Or climb his knees the envied kiss to share.

Oft did the harvest to their sickle yield,
Their furrow oft the stubborn glebe has broke;
How jocund did they drive their team afield!
How bowed the woods beneath their sturdy stroke!

Let not Ambition mock their useful toil,
Their homely joys, and destiny obscure;
Nor Grandeur hear with a disdainful smile
The short and simple annals of the poor.

The boast of heraldry, the pomp of power,
And all that beauty, all that wealth e'er gave,
Await alike the inevitable hour:
The paths of glory lead but to the grave.

Nor you, ye proud, impute to these the fault
If Memory o'er their tomb no trophies raise,
Where through the long-drawn aisle and fretted vault
The pealing anthem swells the note of praise.

Can storied urn or animated bust
Back to its mansion call the fleeting breath?
Can Honour's voice provoke the silent dust,
Or Flattery soothe the dull cold ear of Death?

Perhaps in this neglected spot is laid
Some heart once pregnant with celestial fire;
Hands, that the rod of empire might have swayed,
Or waked to ecstasy the living lyre;

But Knowledge to their eyes her ample page,
Rich with the spoils of time, did ne'er unroll;
Chill Penury repressed their noble rage,
And froze the genial current of the soul.

Full many a gem of purest ray serene
The dark unfathomed caves of ocean bear;
Full many a flower is born to blush unseen,
And waste its sweetness on the desert air.

Some village Hampden, that with dauntless breast
The little tyrant of his fields withstood,
Some mute inglorious Milton here may rest,
Some Cromwell guiltless of his country's blood.

★   ★   ★

Far from the madding crowd's ignoble strife,
Their sober wishes never learned to stray;
Along the cool, sequestered vale of life
They kept the noiseless tenor of their way.

Yet, ev'n these bones from insult to protect,
Some frail memorial still erected nigh,
With uncouth rhimes and shapeless sculpture decked,
Implores the passing tribute of a sigh.

Their name, their years, spelt by the unlettered muse,
The place of fame and elegy supply:
And many a holy text around she strews,
That teach the rustic moralist to die.

For who, to dumb forgetfulness a prey,
This pleasing anxious being e'er resign'd,
Left the warm precincts of the cheerful day,
Nor cast one longing lingering look behind?

On some fond breast the parting soul relies,
Some pious drops the closing eye requires;
Ev'n from the tomb the voice of Nature cries,
Ev'n in our ashes live their wonted fires.

For thee, who, mindful of the unhonoured dead,
Dost in these lines their artless tale relate;
If chance, by lonely contemplation led,
Some kindred spirit shall inquire thy fate,

Haply some hoary-headed swain may say,
"Oft have we seen him at the peep of dawn
Brushing with hasty steps the dews away,
To meet the sun upon the upland lawn;

There at the foot of yonder nodding beech
That wreathes its old fantastic roots so high,
His listless length at noon-tide would he stretch,
And pore upon the brook that babbles by.

Hard by yon wood, now smiling as in scorn,
Muttering his wayward fancies he would rove;
Now drooping, woeful-wan, like one forlorn,
Or crazed with care, or crossed in hopeless love.

One morn I missed him on the customed hill,
Along the heath, and near his favourite tree;
Another came; nor yet beside the rill,
Nor up the lawn, nor at the wood was he;

The next with dirges due in sad array
Slow through the church-way path we saw him borne.
Approach and read (for thou canst read) the lay
Graved on the stone beneath yon aged thorn."

Oliver Goldsmith

From: The Deserted Village

Sweet Auburn! loveliest village of the plain,
Where health and plenty cheered the labouring swain,
Where smiling spring its earliest visit paid,
And parting summer's lingering blooms delayed:
Dear lovely bowers of innocence and ease,
Seats of my youth, when every sport could please,
How often have I loitered o'er thy green,
Where humble happiness endeared each scene;
How often have I paused on every charm,
The sheltered cot, the cultivated farm,
The never-failing brook, the busy mill,
The decent church that topped the neighbouring hill,
The hawthorn bush, with seats beneath the shade,
For talking age and whisp'ring lovers made;
How often have I blessed the coming day,
When toil remitting lent its turn to play,
And all the village train, from labour free,
Led up their sports beneath the spreading tree;
While many a pastime circled in the shade,
The young contending as the old surveyed;

And many a gambol frolicked o'er the ground,
And sleights of art and feats of strength went round;
And still as each repeated pleasure tired,
Succeeding sports the mirthful band inspired;
The dancing pair that simply sought renown,
By holding out to tire each other down;
The swain mistrustless of his smutted face,
While secret laughter tittered round the place;
The bashful virgin's side-long looks of love,
The matron's glance that would those looks reprove,
These were thy charms, sweet village; sports like these,
With sweet succession, taught e'en toil to please;
These round thy bowers their cheerful influence shed,
These were thy charms – But all these charms are fled.

* * *

Sweet was the sound, when oft at evening's close
Up yonder hill the village murmur rose;
There, as I passed with careless steps and slow,
The mingling notes came softened from below;
The swain responsive as the milk-maid sung,
The sober herd that lowed to meet their young;
The noisy geese that gabbled o'er the pool,

The playful children just let loose from school;
The watchdog's voice that bayed the whisp'ring wind,
And the loud laugh that spoke the vacant mind;
These all in sweet confusion sought the shade,
And filled each pause the nightingale had made.
But now the sounds of population fail,
No cheerful murmurs fluctuate in the gale,
No busy steps the grass-grown foot-way tread,
For all the bloomy flush of life is fled.
All but yon widowed, solitary thing
That feebly bends beside the plashy spring;
She, wretched matron, forced, in age, for bread,
To strip the brook with mantling cresses spread,
To pick her wintry faggot from the thorn,
To seek her nightly shed, and weep till morn;
She only left of all the harmless train,
The sad historian of the pensive plain.

WILLIAM COWPER

FROM: THE TASK

I saw the woods and fields at close of day,
A variegated show; the meadows green,
Though faded; and the lands, where lately waved
The golden harvest, of a mellow brown,
Upturned so lately by the forceful share.
I saw far off the weedy fallows smile
With verdure not unprofitable, grazed
By flocks, fast feeding, and selecting each
His favourite herb; while all the leafless groves,
That skirt the horizon, wore a sable hue,
Scarce noticed in the kindred dusk of eve.
To-morrow brings a change, a total change,
Which even now, though silently performed
And slowly, and by most unfelt, the face
Of universal nature undergoes.
Fast falls a fleecy shower: the downy flakes
Descending, and with never-ceasing lapse
Softly alighting upon all below,
Assimilate all objects. Earth receives
Gladly the thickening mantle, and the green

*And tender blade that feared the chilling blast
Escapes unhurt beneath so warm a veil. . . .
Ill fares the traveller now, and he that stalks
In ponderous boots beside his reeking team.
The wain goes heavily, impeded sore
By congregated loads adhering close
To the clogged wheels, and, in its sluggish pace
Noiseless, appears a moving hill of snow.
The toiling steeds expand the nostril wide,
While every breath, by respiration strong
Forced downward, is consolidated soon
Upon their jutting chests. He, formed to bear
The pelting brunt of the tempestuous night,
With half-shut eyes and puckered cheeks, and teeth
Presented bare against the storm, plods on.
One hand secures his hat, save when with both
He brandishes his pliant length of whip,
Resounding oft, and never heard in vain.*

WILLIAM COWPER

THE STREAM
(Addressed to a Young Lady)

Sweet stream, that winds through yonder glade,
Apt emblem of a virtuous maid:
Silent and chaste she steals along,
Far from the world's gay busy throng,
With gentle yet prevailing force,
Intent upon her destined course;
Graceful and useful all she does,
Blessing and blest where'er she goes,
Pure-bosomed as that watery glass,
And heaven reflected in her face.

Anna Letitia Barbauld

Ode to Spring

Sweet daughter of a rough and stormy sire,
Hoar Winter's blooming child, delightful Spring!
  Whose unshorn locks with leaves
  And swelling buds are crowned;

From the green islands of eternal youth
(Crowned with fresh blooms, and ever-springing shade)
  Turn, hither turn thy step,
  O thou, whose powerful voice,

More sweet than softest touch of Doric reed,
Or Lydian flute, can soothe the madding winds,
  And through the stormy deep
  Breathe thine own tender calm.

Thee, best beloved! the virgin train await
With songs and festal rites, and joy to rove
  Thy blooming wilds among,
  And vales and dewy lawns,

With untired feet; and cull thy earliest sweet,
To weave fresh garlands for the glowing brow
   Of him, the favoured youth
   That prompts their whispered sigh.

Unlock thy copious stores, – those tender showers
That drop their sweetness on the infant buds;
   And silent dews that swell
   The milky ear's green stem,

And feed the flowering osier's early shoots;
And call those winds which through the whispering
   boughs
   With warm and pleasant breath
   Salute the bowing flowers.

Now let me sit beneath the whitening thorn
And mark thy spreading tints steal o'er the dale,
   And watch with patient eye
   Thy fair unfolding charms.

O nymph, approach! while yet the temperate sun
With bashful forehead through the cool moist air
   Throws his young maiden beams,
   And with chaste kisses woos

*The earth's fair bosom; while the streaming veil
Of lucid clouds with wind and frequent shade
   Protects thy modest blooms
   From his severer blaze.*

*Sweet is thy reign, but short: the red dog-star
Shall scorch thy tresses, and the mower's scythe
   Thy greens, thy flowerets all,
   Remorseless shall destroy.*

*Reluctant shall I bid thee then farewell;
For O! not all that Autumn's lap contains,
   Nor Summer's ruddiest fruits,
   Can aught for thee atone,*

*Fair Spring! whose simplest promise more delights,
Then all their largest wealth, and through the heart
   Each joy and new-born hope
   With softest influence breathes.*

George Crabbe

Birds in Winter

High o'er the restless deep, above the reach
Of gunner's hope, vast flights of wild-ducks stretch;
Far as the eye can glance on either side,
In a broad space and level line they glide;
All in their wedge-like figures from the north,
Day after day, flight after flight, go forth.
   In-shore, their passage tribes of sea-gulls urge
And drop for prey within the sweeping surge;
Oft in the rough opposing blast they fly
Far back, then turn, and all their force apply,
While to the storm they give their weak complaining cry,
Or clap the sleek white pinion to the breast,
And in the restless ocean dip for rest.

William Blake

The Shepherd

How sweet is the shepherd's sweet lot!
From the morn to the evening he strays;
He shall follow his sheep all the day,
And his tongue shall be fillèd with praise.

For he hears the lambs' innocent call,
And he hears the ewes' tender reply:
He is watchful while they are in peace,
For they know when their shepherd is nigh.

JOANNA BAILLIE

From: Hay Making

Upon the grass no longer hangs the dew;
Forth hies the mower, with his glittering scythe,
In snowy shirt bedight, and all unbraced,
He moves athwart the mead with sidling bend,
And lays the grass in many a swathey line:
In every field, in every lawn and meadow,
The rousing voice of industry is heard;
The haycock rises, and the frequent rake
Sweeps on the fragrant hay in heavy wreaths.
The old and young, the weak and strong, are there,
And, as they can, help on the cheerful work.

* * *

Some, more advanced, raise up the lofty rick,
Whilst on its top doth stand the parish toast,
In loose attire, and swelling ruddy cheek.
With taunts and harmless mockery she receives
The tossed-up heaps from fork of simple youth,
Who, staring on her, takes his arm away,

While half the load falls back upon himself.
Loud is her laugh, her voice is heard afar:
The mower busied on the distant lawn,
The carter trudging on his dusty way,
The shrill sound know, their bonnets toss in air,
And roar across the field to catch her notice:
She waves her arm to them, and shakes her head,
And then renews her work with double spirit.
Thus do they jest and laugh away their toil
Till the bright sun, now past his middle course,
Shoots down his fiercest beams which none may brave.
The stoutest arm feels listless, and the swart
And brawny-shouldered clown begins to fail,
But to the weary, lo! there comes relief!
A troop of welcome children o'er the lawn
With slow and wary steps approach: some bear
In baskets oaten cakes or barley scones,
And gusty cheese and stoups of milk or whey.
Beneath the branches of a spreading tree,
Or by the shady side of the tall rick,
They spread their homely fare, and seated round,
Taste every pleasure that a feast can give.

WILLIAM WORDSWORTH

From: Lines
Composed a Few Miles above Tintern Abbey, on Revisiting the Banks of the Wye During a Tour. July 13, 1798

Five years have past; five summers, with the length
Of five long winters! and again I hear
These waters, rolling from their mountain-springs
With a soft inland murmur. – Once again
Do I behold these steep and lofty cliffs,
That on a wild secluded scene impress
Thoughts of more deep seclusion; and connect
The landscape with the quiet of the sky.
The day is come when I again repose
Here, under this dark sycamore, and view
These plots of cottage-ground, these orchard-tufts,
Which at this season, with their unripe fruits,
Are clad in one green hue, and lose themselves
'Mid groves and copses. Once again I see
These hedge-rows, hardly hedge-rows, little lines
Of sportive wood run wild: these pastoral farms,
Green to the very door; and wreaths of smoke

Sent up, in silence, from among the trees!
With some uncertain notice, as might seem
Of vagrant dwellers in the houseless woods,
Or of some Hermit's cave, where by his fire
The Hermit sits alone.
    These beauteous forms,
Through a long absence, have not been to me
As is a landscape to a blind man's eye:
But oft, in lonely rooms, and 'mid the din
Of towns and cities, I have owed to them,
In hours of weariness, sensations sweet,
Felt in the blood, and felt along the heart;
And passing even into my purer mind,
With tranquil restoration: – feelings too
Of unremembered pleasure: such, perhaps,
As have no slight or trivial influence
On that best portion of a good man's life,
His little, nameless, unremembered, acts
Of kindness and of love. Nor less, I trust,
To them I may have owed another gift,
Of aspect more sublime; that blessed mood,
In which the burthen of the mystery,
In which the heavy and the weary weight
Of all this unintelligible world,

Is lightened: – that serene and blessed mood,
In which the affections gently lead us on, –
Until, the breath of this corporeal frame
And even the motion of our human blood
Almost suspended, we are laid asleep
In body, and become a living soul:
While with an eye made quiet by the power
Of harmony, and the deep power of joy,
We see into the life of things.

* * *

And now, with gleams of half-extinguished thought,
With many recognitions dim and faint,
And somewhat of a sad perplexity,
The picture of the mind revives again:
While here I stand, not only with the sense
Of present pleasure, but with pleasing thoughts
That in this moment there is life and food
For future years. And so I dare to hope,
Though changed, no doubt, from what I was when first
I came among these hills; when like a roe
I bounded o'er the mountains, by the sides
Of the deep rivers, and the lonely streams,

Wherever nature led: more like a man
Flying from something that he dreads than one
Who sought the thing he loved. For nature then
(The coarser pleasures of my boyish days,
And their glad animal movements all gone by)
To me was all in all. – I cannot paint
What then I was. The sounding cataract
Haunted me like a passion: the tall rock,
The mountain, and the deep and gloomy wood,
Their colours and their forms, were then to me
An appetite; a feeling and a love,
That had no need of a remoter charm,
By thought supplied, nor any interest
Unborrowed from the eye. – That time is past,
And all its aching joys are now no more,
And all its dizzy raptures. Not for this
Faint I, nor mourn nor murmur; other gifts
Have followed; for such loss, I would believe,
Abundant recompense. For I have learned
To look on nature, not as in the hour
Of thoughtless youth; but hearing oftentimes
The still, sad music of humanity,
Nor harsh nor grating, though of ample power
To chasten and subdue. And I have felt

*A presence that disturbs me with the joy
Of elevated thoughts; a sense sublime
Of something far more deeply interfused,
Whose dwelling is the light of setting suns,
And the round ocean and the living air,
And the blue sky, and in the mind of man:
A motion and a spirit, that impels
All thinking things, all objects of all thought,
And rolls through all things. Therefore am I still
A lover of the meadows and the woods,
And mountains; and of all that we behold
From this green earth; of all the mighty world
Of eye, and ear, – both what they half create,
And what perceive; well pleased to recognise
In nature and the language of the sense
The anchor of my purest thoughts, the nurse,
The guide, the guardian of my heart, and soul
Of all my moral being.*

* * *

*. . . Nor, perchance –
If I should be where I no more can hear
Thy voice, nor catch from thy wild eyes these gleams*

Of past existence – wilt thou then forget
That on the banks of this delightful stream
We stood together; and that I, so long
A worshipper of Nature, hither came
Unwearied in that service: rather say
With warmer love – oh! with far deeper zeal
Of holier love. Nor wilt thou then forget
That after many wanderings, many years
Of absence, these steep woods and lofty cliffs,
And this green pastoral landscape, were to me
More dear, both for themselves and for thy sake!

William Wordsworth

The Solitary Reaper

*Behold her, single in the field,
Yon solitary Highland Lass!
Reaping, and singing by herself;
Stop here, or gently pass!
Alone she cuts and binds the grain,
And sings a melancholy strain;
O listen! for the Vale profound
Is overflowing with the sound.*

*No Nightingale did ever chaunt
More welcome notes to weary bands
Of travellers in some shady haunt,
Among Arabian sands:
A voice so thrilling ne'er was heard
In spring-time from the Cuckoo-bird,
Breaking the silence of the seas
Among the farthest Hebrides.*

Will no one tell me what she sings? –
Perhaps the plaintive numbers flow
For old, unhappy, far-off things,
And battles long ago:
Or is it some more humble lay,
Familiar matter of to-day?
Some natural sorrow, loss, or pain,
That has been, and may be again?

Whate'er the theme, the Maiden sang
As if her song could have no ending;
I saw her singing at her work,
And o'er the sickle bending; –
I listened, motionless and still;
And, as I mounted up the hill,
The music in my heart I bore,
Long after it was heard no more.

WILLIAM WORDSWORTH

THE DAFFODILS

I wandered lonely as a cloud
  That floats on high o'er vales and hills,
When all at once I saw a crowd,
  A host, of golden daffodils,
Beside the lake, beneath the trees,
Fluttering and dancing in the breeze.

Continuous as the stars that shine
  And twinkle on the milky way,
They stretched in never-ending line
  Along the margin of a bay:
Ten thousand saw I at a glance
Tossing their heads in sprightly dance.

The waves beside them danced, but they
  Out-did the sparkling waves in glee:
A Poet could not but be gay
  In such a jocund company!
I gazed – and gazed – but little thought
What wealth the show to me had brought:

For oft, when on my couch I lie
   In vacant or in pensive mood,
They flash upon that inward eye
   Which is the bliss of solitude;
And then my heart with pleasure fills,
And dances with the daffodils.

Samuel Taylor Coleridge

To Nature

It may indeed be phantasy, when I
 Essay to draw from all created things
 Deep, heartfelt, inward joy that closely clings;
And trace in leaves and flowers that round me lie
Lessons of love and earnest piety.
 So let it be; and if the wide world rings
 In mock of this belief, it brings
Nor fear, nor grief, nor vain perplexity.
So will I build my altar in the fields,
 And the blue sky my fretted dome shall be,
And the sweet fragrance that the wild flower yields
 Shall be the incense I will yield to Thee,
Thee only God! and thou shalt not despise
Even me, the priest of this poor sacrifice.

Ebenezer Elliot

Spring

Again the violet of our early days
Drinks beauteous azure from the golden sun,
And kindles into fragrance at his blaze;
The streams, rejoiced that winter's work is done,
Talk of to-morrow's cowslips, as they run.
Wild apple, thou art bursting into bloom!
Thy leaves are coming, snowy-blossomed thorn!
Wake, buried lily! spirit, quit thy tomb;
And thou, shade-loving hyacinth, be born!
Then, haste, sweet rose! sweet woodbine, hymn the morn,
Whose dew-drops shall illume with pearly light
Each grassy blade that thick embattled stands
From sea to sea, while daisies infinite
Uplift in praise their little glowing hands,
O'er every hill that under heaven expands.

Percy Bysshe Shelley

Summer and Winter

It was a bright and cheerful afternoon,
Towards the end of the sunny month of June,
When the north wind congregates in crowds
The floating mountains of the silver clouds
From the horizon – and the stainless sky
Opens beyond them like eternity.
All things rejoiced beneath the sun; the weeds,
The river, and the corn-fields, and the reeds;
The willow leaves that glanced in the light breeze,
And the firm foliage of the larger trees.

It was a winter such as when birds die
In the deep forests; and the fishes lie
Stiffened in the translucent ice, which makes
Even the mud and slime of the warm lakes
A wrinkled clod as hard as brick; and when,
Among their children, comfortable men
Gather about great fires, and yet feel cold:
Alas, then, for the homeless beggar old!

Percy Bysshe Shelley

Ode to the West Wind

(i)

O wild West Wind, thou breath of Autumn's being,
    Thou, from whose unseen presence the leaves dead
Are driven, like ghosts from an enchanter fleeing,

Yellow, and black, and pale, and hectic red,
    Pestilence-stricken multitudes: O thou
Who chariotest to their dark wintry bed

The wingèd seeds, where they lie cold and low,
    Each like a corpse within its grave, until
Thine azure sister of the Spring shall blow

Her clarion o'er the dreaming earth, and fill
    (Driving sweet buds like flocks to feed in air)
With living hues and odours plain and hill:

Wild Sprit, which art moving everywhere;
Destroyer and Preserver; hear, O hear!

(ii)

Thou on whose stream, 'mid the steep sky's commotion,
  Loose clouds like earth's decaying leaves are shed,
Shook from the tangled boughs of heaven and ocean,

Angels of rain and lightning: there are spread
  On the blue surface of thine airy surge,
Like the bright hair uplifted from the head

Of some fierce Maenad, even from the dim verge
  Of the horizon to the zenith's height,
The locks of the approaching storm. Thou dirge

Of the dying year, to which this closing night
  Will be the dome of a vast sepulchre,
Vaulted with all thy congregated might

Of vapours, from whose solid atmosphere
Black rain, and fire, and hail, will burst: oh hear!

(iii)

Thou who didst waken from his summer dreams
  The blue Mediterranean, where he lay,
Lulled by the coil of his crystálline streams

Beside a pumice isle in Baiae's bay,
    And saw in sleep old palaces and towers
Quivering within the wave's intenser day,

All overgrown with azure moss and flowers
    So sweet, the sense faints picturing them! Thou
For whose path the Atlantic's level powers

Cleave themselves into chasms, while far below
    The sea-blooms and the oozy woods which wear
The sapless foliage of the ocean, know

Thy voice, and suddenly grow grey with fear,
And tremble and despoil themselves: oh hear!

(iv)

If I were a dead leaf thou mightest bear;
    If I were a swift cloud to fly with thee;
A wave to pant beneath thy power, and share

The impulse of thy strength, only less free
    Than thou, O uncontrollable! If even
I were as in my boyhood, and could be

The comrade of thy wanderings over heaven,
    As then, when to outstrip thy skiey speed
Scarce seemed a vision, I would ne'er have striven

As thus with thee in prayer in my sore need.
    O, lift me as a wave, a leaf, a cloud!
I fall upon the thorns of life! I bleed!

A heavy weight of hours has chained and bowed
One too like thee: tameless, and swift, and proud.

(v)

Make me thy lyre, even as the forest is:
    What if my leaves are falling like its own!
The tumult of thy mighty harmonies

Will take from both a deep autumnal tone,
    Sweet though in sadness. Be thou, Spirit fierce,
My spirit! Be thou me, impetuous one!

Drive my dead-thoughts over the universe
    Like withered leaves to quicken a new birth!
And, by the incantation of this verse,

Scatter, as from an unextinguished hearth
    Ashes and sparks, my words among mankind!
Be through my lips to unawakened earth

The trumpet of a prophecy! O Wind,
If Winter comes, can Spring be far behind?

John Clare

The Shepherd's Tree

Huge elm, with rifted trunk all notched and scarred,
Like to a warrior's destiny, I love
To stretch me often on thy shadowed sward,
And hear the laugh of summer leaves above;
Or on thy buttressed roots to sit, and lean
In careless attitude, and there reflect
On times and deeds and darings that have been –
Old castaways, now swallowed in neglect, –
While thou art towering in thy strength of heart,
Stirring the soul to vain imaginings
In which life's sordid being hath no part.
The wind of that eternal ditty sings,
  Humming of future things, that burn the mind
  To leave some fragment of itself behind.

John Clare

Autumn

*The thistle down's flying, though the winds are all still,
On the green grass now lying, now mounting the hill,
The spring from the fountain now boils like a pot;
Through stones past the counting it bubbles red-hot.*

*The ground parched and cracked is like overbaked bread,
The greensward all wracked is, bents dried up and dead.
The fallow fields glitter like water indeed,
And gossamers twitter, flung from weed unto weed.*

*Hill tops like hot iron glitter bright in the sun,
And the rivers we're eying burn to gold as they run;
Burning hot is the ground, liquid gold is the air;
Whoever looks round sees Eternity there.*

JOHN KEATS

TO AUTUMN

Season of mists and mellow fruitfulness
  Close bosom-friend of the maturing sun;
Conspiring with him how to load and bless
  With fruit the vines that round the thatch-eves run;
To bend with apples the moss'd cottage-trees,
  And fill all fruit with ripeness to the core;
    To swell the gourd, and plump the hazel shells
  With a sweet kernel; to set budding more,
And still more, later flowers for the bees,
Until they think warm days will never cease,
    For Summer has o'er-brimm'd their clammy cells.

Who hath not seen thee oft amid thy store?
  Sometimes whoever seeks abroad may find
Thee sitting careless on a granary floor,
  Thy hair soft-lifted by the winnowing wind;
Or on a half-reap'd furrow sound asleep,
  Drows'd with the fume of poppies, while thy hook
    Spares the next swath and all its twined flowers:
And sometimes like a gleaner thou dost keep

Steady thy laden head across a brook;
Or by a cyder-press, with patient look,
    Thou watchest the last oozings hours by hours.

Where are the songs of Spring? Ay, where are they?
    Think not of them, thou hast thy music too, –
While barred clouds bloom the soft-dying day,
    And touch the stubble-plains with rosy hue;
Then in a wailful choir the small gnats mourn
    Among the river sallows, borne aloft
        Or sinking as the light wind lives or dies;
And full-grown lambs loud bleat from hilly bourn;
    Hedge-crickets sing; and now with treble soft
    The red-breast whistles from a garden-croft;
        And gathering swallows twitter in the skies.

JOHN KEATS

FROM: ENDYMION

A thing of beauty is a joy for ever:
Its loveliness increases; it will never
Pass into nothingness; but still will keep
A bower quiet for us, and a sleep
Full of sweet dreams, and health, and quiet breathing.
Therefore, on every morrow, are we wreathing
A flowery band to bind us to the earth,
Spite of despondence, of the inhuman dearth
Of noble natures, of the gloomy days,
Of all the unhealthy and o'er-darkened ways
Made for our searching: yes, in spite of all,
Some shape of beauty moves away the pall
From our dark spirits. Such the sun, the moon,
Trees old, and young, sprouting a shady boon
For simple sheep; and such are daffodils
With the green world they live in; and clear rills
That for themselves a cooling covert make
'Gainst the hot season; the mid forest brake,
Rich with a sprinkling of fair musk-rose blooms:
And such too is the grandeur of the dooms

We have imagined for the mighty dead;
All lovely tales that we have heard or read:
And endless fountain of immortal drink,
Pouring unto us from the heaven's brink.

Thomas Hood

From: Autumn

I saw old Autumn in the misty morn
Stand shadowless like Silence, listening
To silence, for no lonely birds would sing
Into his hollow ear from woods forlorn,
Nor lowly hedge nor solitary thorn: –
Shaking his languid locks all dewy bright
With tangled gossamer that fell by night,
   Pearling his coronet of golden corn.

Where are the songs of Summer? – With the sun,
Oping the dusky eyelids of the south,
Till shade and silence waken up as one,
And Morning sings with a warm odorous mouth.
Where are the merry birds? – Away, away,
On panting wings through the inclement skies,
    Lest owls should prey
    Undazzled at noonday,
And tear with horny beak their lustrous eyes.

Where are the blooms of Summer? – In the west,
Blushing their last to the last sunny hours,
When the mild Eve by sudden Night is prest
Like tearful Proserpine, snatched from her flowers
    To a most gloomy breast.
Where is the pride of Summer, – the green prime, –
The many, many leaves all twinkling? – Three
On the mossed elm; three on the naked lime
Trembling, – and one upon the old oak-tree!
    Where is the Dryad's immortality? –
Gone into mournful cypress and dark yew,
Or wearing the long gloomy Winter through
    In the smooth holly's green eternity.

Elizabeth Barrett Browning

From: Aurora Leigh

Whoever lives true life, will love true love.
I learnt to love that England. Very oft,
Before the day was born, or otherwise
Through secret windings of the afternoons,
I threw my hunters off and plunged myself
Among the deep hills, as a hunted stag
Will take the waters, shivering with the fear
And passion of the course. And when at last
Escaped, so many a green slope built on slope
Betwixt me and the enemy's house behind,
I dared to rest, or wander, in a rest
Made sweeter for the step upon the grass,
And view the ground's most gentle dimplement
(As if God's finger touched but did not press
In making England), such an up and down
Of verdure, – nothing too much up or down,
A ripple of land; such little hills, the sky
Can stoop to tenderly and the wheat-fields climb;
Such nooks of valleys lined with orchises,
Fed full of noises by invisible streams;

*And open pastures where you scarcely tell
White daisies from white dew, – at intervals
The mythic oaks and elm-trees standing out
Self-poised upon their prodigy of shade, –
I thought my father's land was worthy too
Of being my Shakespeare's.*

* * *

*But then the thrushes sang,
And shook my pulses and elms' new leaves;
At which I turned, and held my finger up,
And bade him mark that, howsoe'er the world
Went ill, as he related, certainly
The thrushes still sang in it. At the word
His brow would soften, – and he bore with me
In melancholy patience, not unkind,
While breaking into voluble ecstasy
I flattered all the beauteous country round,
As poets use, the skies, the clouds, the fields,
The happy violets hiding from the roads
The primroses run down to, carrying gold;
The tangled hedgerows, where the cows push out
Impatient horns and tolerant churning mouths*

*'Twixt dripping ash-boughs, – hedgerows all alive
With birds and gnats and large white butterflies
Which look as if the May-flower had caught life
And palpitated forth upon the wind;
Hills, vales, woods, netted in a silver mist,
Farms, granges, doubled up among the hills;
And cattle grazing in the watered vales,
And cottage-chimneys smoking from the woods,
And cottage-gardens smelling everywhere,
Confused with smell of orchards.*

ALFRED, LORD TENNYSON

FROM: IN MEMORIAM

(i)

Calm is the morn without a sound,
    Calm as to suit a calmer grief,
    And only through the faded leaf
The chestnut pattering to the ground:

Calm and deep peace on this high wold,
    And on these dews that drench the furze,
    And all the silvery gossamers
That twinkle into green and gold:

Calm and still light on yon great plain
    That sweeps with all its autumn bowers,
    And crowded farms and lessening towers,
To mingle with the bounding main:

Calm and deep peace in this wide air,
    These leaves that redden to the fall;
    And in my heart, if calm at all,
If any calm, a calm despair:

Calm on the seas, and silver sleep,
    And waves that sway themselves in rest,
    And dead calm in that noble breast
Which heaves but with the heaving deep.

(ii)

The wish, that of the living whole
    No life may fail beyond the grave,
    Derives it not from what we have
The likest God within the soul?

Are God and Nature then at strife,
    That Nature lends such evil dreams?
    So careful of the type she seems,
So careless of the single life;

That I, considering everywhere
    Her secret meaning in her deeds,
    And finding that of fifty seeds
She often brings but one to bear,

I falter where I firmly trod,
    And falling with my weight of cares
    Upon the great world's altar-stairs
That slope through darkness up to God,

I stretch lame hands of faith, and grope,
 And gather dust and chaff, and call
 To what I feel is Lord of all,
And faintly trust the larger hope.

(iii)

Now fades the last long streak of snow,
 Now burgeons every maze of quick
 About the flowering squares, and thick
By ashen roots the violets blow.

Now rings the woodland loud and long,
 The distance takes a lovelier hue,
 And drowned in yonder living blue
The lark becomes a sightless song.

Now dance the lights on lawn and lea,
 The flocks are whiter down the vale,
 And milkier every milky sail
On winding stream or distant sea;

Where now the seamew pipes, or dives
 In yonder greening gleam, and fly
 The happy birds, that change their sky
To build and brood; that live their lives

From land to land; and in my breast
  Spring wakens too; and my regret
  Becomes an April violet,
And buds and blossoms like the rest.

(iv)

There rolls the deep where grew the tree.
  O earth, what changes hast thou seen!
  There where the long street roars, hath been
The stillness of the central sea.

The hills are shadows, and they flow
  From form to form, and nothing stands;
  They melt like mist, the solid lands,
Like clouds they shape themselves and go.

But in my spirit will I dwell,
  And dream my dream, and hold it true;
  For though my lips may breathe adieu,
I cannot think the thing farewell.

ROBERT BROWNING

THE YEAR'S AT THE SPRING

The year's at the spring,
And day's at the morn;
Morning's at seven;
The hill-side's dew-pearled;
The lark's on the wing;
The snail's on the thorn;
God's in His Heaven –
All's right with the world!

HOME THOUGHTS, FROM ABROAD

O to be in England
Now that April's there.
And whoever wakes in England
Sees, some morning, unaware,
That the lowest boughs and the brushwood sheaf
Round the elm-tree bole are in tiny leaf,

While the chaffinch sings on the orchard bough
In England – now!
And after April, when May follows,
And the whitethroat builds, and all the swallows!
Hark, where my blossom'd pear-tree in the hedge
Leans to the field and scatters on the clover
Blossoms and dewdrops – at the bent spray's edge –
That's the wise thrush; he sings each song twice over,
Lest you should think he never could recapture
The first fine careless rapture!
And though the fields look rough with hoary dew,
All will be gay when noontide wakes anew
The buttercups, the little children's dower
– Far brighter than this gaudy melon-flower!

Dante Gabriel Rossetti

Silent Noon

Your hands lie open in the long fresh grass, –
  The finger-points look through like rosy blooms:
  Your eyes smile peace. The pasture gleams and
    glooms
'Neath billowing skies that scatter and amass.
All round our nest, far as the eye can pass,
  Are golden kingcup-fields with silver edge
  Where the cow-parsley skirts the hawthorn-hedge.
'Tis visible silence, still as the hour-glass.

Deep in the sun-searched growths the dragon-fly
Hangs like a blue-thread loosened from the sky: –
  So this wing'd hour is dropt to us from above.
Oh! clasp we to our hearts, for deathless dower,
This close-companioned inarticulate hour
  When two-fold silence was the song of love.

GEORGE MEREDITH

WE SAW THE SWALLOWS ...

We saw the swallows gathering in the sky,
And in the osier-isle we heard their noise.
We had not to look back on Summer joys,
Or forward to a Summer of bright dye:
But in the largeness of the evening earth
Our spirits grew as we went side by side.
The hour became her husband, and my bride.
Love, that had robbed us so, thus blessed our dearth!
The pilgrims of the year waxed very loud
In multitudinous chatterings, as the flood
Full brown came from the West, and like pale blood
Expanded to the upper crimson cloud.
Love, that had robbed us of immortal things,
This little moment mercifully gave,
Where I have seen across the twilight wave
The swan sail with her young beneath her wings.

Christina Rossetti

Spring Quiet

Gone were but the Winter,
    Come were but the Spring.
I would go to a covert
    Where the birds sing;

Where in the whitethorn
    Singeth a thrush,
And a robin sings
    In the holly-bush.

Full of fresh scents
    Are the budding boughs
Arching high over
    A cool green house;

Full of sweet scents,
    And whispering air
Which sayeth softly:
    "We spread no snare;

"Here dwell in safety,
    Here dwell alone,
With a clear stream
    And a mossy stone.

"Here the sun shinest
    Most shadily;
Here is heard an echo
    Of the far sea,
    Though far off it be."

Thomas Hardy

Afterwards

When the Present has latched its postern behind my
   tremulous stay,
And the May month flaps its glad green leaves like
   wings,
Delicate-filmed as new-spun silk, will the neighbours
   say,
"He was a man who used to notice such things"?

If it be in the dusk when, like an eyelid's soundless
   blink,
The dewfall-hawk comes crossing the shades to alight
Upon the wind-warped upland thorn, a gazer may
   think,
"To him this must have been a familiar sight."

If I pass during some nocturnal blackness, mothy and
   warm,
When the hedgehog travels furtively over the lawn,
One may say, "He strove that such innocent creatures
   should come to no harm,
But he could do little for them; and now he is gone."

*If, when hearing that I have been stilled at last, they
  stand at the door,*
Watching the full-starred heavens that winter sees,
*Will this thought rise on those who will meet my face no
  more,*
"He was one who had an eye for such mysteries"?

*And will any say when my bell of quittance is heard in
  the gloom,*
And a crossing breeze cuts a pause in its outrollings,
Till they rise again, as they were a new bell's boom,
"He hears it not now, but used to notice such things"?

GERARD MANLEY HOPKINS

THE WINDHOVER:

To Christ our Lord

I caught this morning morning's minion, king-
   dom of daylight's dauphin, dapple-dawn-drawn
      Falcon, in his riding
   Of the rolling level underneath him steady air, and
      striding
High there, how he rung upon the rein of a wimpling
      wing
In his ecstasy! then off, off forth on swing,
   As a skate's heel sweeps smooth on a bow-bend: the
      hurl and gliding
   Rebuffed the big wind. My heart in hiding
Stirred for a bird, – the achieve of, the mastery of the
      thing!

Brute beauty and valour and act, oh, air, pride, plume, here
   Buckle! AND *the fire that breaks from thee then, a billion*
Times told lovelier, more dangerous, O my chevalier!
   No wonder of it: sheér plód makes plough down sillion
Shine, and blue-bleak embers, ah my dear,
   Fall, gall themselves, and gash gold-vermilion.

GERARD MANLEY HOPKINS

PIED BEAUTY

Glory be to God for dappled things –
 For skies of couple-colour as a brinded cow;
  For rose-moles all in stipple upon trout that swim;
Fresh-firecoal chestnut-falls; finches' wings;
 Landscape plotted and pieced – fold, fallow, and
  plough;
  And, áll trádes, their gear and tackle and trim.

All things counter, original, spare, strange;
 Whatever is fickle, freckled (who knows how?)
  What swift, slow; sweet, sour; adazzle, dim;
He fathers-forth whose beauty is past change:
            Praise him.

Gerard Manley Hopkins

Spring

Nothing is so beautiful as spring –
When weeds, in wheels, shoot long and lovely and lush;
Thrush's eggs look little low heavens, and thrush
Through the echoing timber does so rinse and wring
The ear, it strikes like lightnings to hear him sing;
The glassy peartree leaves and blooms, they brush
The descending blue; that blue is all in a rush
With richness; the racing lambs too have fair their fling.

What is all this juice and all this joy?
A strain of the earth's sweet being in the beginning
In Eden garden. – Have, get, before it cloy,
Before it cloud, Christ, lord, and sour with sinning.
Innocent mind and Mayday in girl and boy,
Most, O maid's child, thy choice and worthy the winning.

ROBERT BRIDGES

FROM: NOVEMBER

   Out by the ricks the mantled engine stands
Crestfallen, deserted, – for now all hands
Are told to the plough, – and ere it is dawn appear
The teams following and crossing far and near,
As hour by hour they broaden the brown bands
Of the striped fields; and behind them firk and prance
The heavy rooks, and daws grey-pated dance:
As awhile, surmounting a crest, in sharp outline
(A miniature of toil, a gem's design,)
They are pictured, horses and men, or now near by
Above the lane they shout lifting the share,
By the trim hedgerow bloom'd with purple air;
Where, under the thorns, dead leaves in huddle lie
Packed by the gales of Autumn, and in and out
The small wrens glide
With a happy note of cheer,
And yellow amorets flutter above and about,
Gay, familiar in fear.

* * *

And here and there, near chilly setting of sun,
In an isolated tree a congregation
Of starlings chatter and chide,
Thickset as summer leaves, in garrulous quarrel:
Suddenly they hush as one, –
The tree top springs, –
And off, with a whirr of wings,
They fly by the score
To the holly-thicket, and there with myriads more
Dispute for the roosts; and from the unseen nation
A babel of tongues, like running water unceasing,
Makes live the wood, the flocking cries increasing,
Wrangling discordantly, incessantly,
While falls the night on them self-occupied;
The long dark night, that lengthens slow,
Deepening with Winter to starve grass and tree,
And soon to bury in snow
The Earth, that, sleeping 'neath her frozen stole,
Shall dream a dream crept from the sunless pole
Of how her end shall be.

A. E. Housman

From: A Shropshire Lad

On Wenlock Edge the wood's in trouble;
His forest fleece the Wrekin heaves;
The gale, it plies the saplings double,
And thick on Severn snow the leaves.

'Twould blow like this through holt and hanger
When Uricon the city stood:
'Tis the old wind in the old anger,
But then it threshed another wood.

Then, 'twas before my time, the Roman
At yonder heaving hill would stare:
The blood that warms an English yeoman,
The thoughts that hurt him, they were there.

There, like the wind through woods in riot,
Through him the gale of life blew high;
The tree of man was never quiet:
Then 'twas the Roman, now 'tis I.

The gale, it plies the saplings double,
It blows so hard, 'twill soon be gone:
To-day the Roman and his trouble
Are ashes under Uricon.

Into my heart an air that kills
From yon far country blows:
What are those blue remembered hills,
What spires, what farms are those?

That is the land of lost content,
I see it shining plain,
The happy highways where I went
And cannot come again.

A. E. Housman

Loveliest of Trees, the Cherry Now

Loveliest of trees, the cherry now
Is hung with bloom along the bough,
And stands about the woodland ride
Wearing white for Eastertide.

Now, of my threescore years and ten,
Twenty will not come again,
And take from seventy springs a score,
It only leaves me fifty more.

And since to look at things in bloom
Fifty springs are little room,
About the woodlands I will go
To see the cherry hung with snow.

Rudyard Kipling

The Way Through the Woods

They shut the road through the woods
Seventy years ago.
Weather and rain have undone it again,
And now you would never know
There was once a road through the woods
Before they planted the trees.
It is underneath the coppice and heath
And the thin anemones.
Only the keeper sees
That, where the ring-dove broods,
And the badgers roll at ease,
There was once a road through the woods.
Yet, if you enter the woods
Of a summer evening late,
When the night-air cools on the trout-ringed pools
Where the otter whistles his mate,
(They fear not men in the woods,
Because they see so few.)
You will hear the beat of a horse's feet,
And the swish of a skirt in the dew,

Steadily cantering through
The misty solitudes,
As though they perfectly knew
The old lost road through the woods . . .
But there is no road through the woods.

From: A Charm

Take of English flowers these –
Spring's full-facèd primroses,
Summer's wild wide-hearted rose,
Autumn's wall-flower of the close,
And, thy darkness to illume,
Winter's bee-thronged ivy-bloom.
Seek and serve them where they bide
From Candlemas to Christmas-tide,
   For these simples, used aright,
   Can restore a failing sight.

W. B. Yeats

The Lake Isle of Innisfree

I will arise and go now, and go to Innisfree,
And a small cabin build there, of clay and wattles made:
Nine bean-rows will I have there, a hive for the honey-
   bee,
And live alone in the bee-loud glade.

And I shall have some peace there, for peace comes
   dropping slow,
Dropping from the veils of the morning to where the
   cricket sings;
There midnight's all a glimmer, and noon a purple
   glow,
And evening full of the linnet's wings.

I will arise and go now, for always night and day
I hear lake water lapping with low sounds by the shore;
While I stand on the roadway, or on the pavements grey,
I hear it in the deep heart's core.

W. B. Yeats

The Wild Swans at Coole

The trees are in their autumn beauty,
The woodland paths are dry,
Under the October twilight the water
Mirrors a still sky;
Upon the brimming water among the stones
Are nine and fifty swans.

The nineteenth Autumn has come upon me
Since I first made my count;
I saw, before I had well finished,
All suddenly mount
And scatter wheeling in great broken rings
Upon their clamorous wings.

I have looked upon those brilliant creatures.
And now my heart is sore,
All's changed since I, hearing at twilight,
The first time on this shore,
The bell-beat of their wings above my head,
Trod with a lighter tread.

Unwearied still, lover by lover,
They paddle in the cold,
Companionable streams or climb the air:
Their hearts have not grown old;
Passion or conquest, wander where they will,
Attend upon them still.

But now they drift on the still water,
Mysterious, beautiful;
Among what rushes will they build,
By what lake's edge or pool
Delight men's eyes when I awake some day
To find they have flown away?

Charlotte Mew

In the Fields

Lord, when I look at lovely things which pass,
Under old trees the shadows of young leaves
Dancing to please the wind along the grass,
Or the gold stillness of the August sun on the August
    sheaves;
Can I believe there is a heavenlier world than this?
And if there is
Will the strange heart of any everlasting thing
Bring me these dreams that take my breath away?
They come at evening with the home-flying rooks and
    the scent of hay,
Over the fields. They come in Spring.

Charlotte Mew

The Trees are Down

– and he cried with a loud voice:
Hurt not the earth, neither the sea, nor the trees –
(Revelation)

*They are cutting down the great plane-trees at the end of
    the gardens.*
*For days there has been the grate of the saw, the swish of
    the branches as they fall,*
The crash of the trunks, the rustle of trodden leaves,
*With the 'Whoops' and the 'Whoas,' the loud common
    talk, the loud common laughs of the
    men, above it all.*

I remember one evening of a long past Spring
*Turning in at a gate, getting out of a cart, and finding a
    large dead rat in the mud of the drive.*
*I remember thinking: alive or dead, a rat was a god-
    forsaken thing,*
But at least, in May, that even a rat should be alive.

*The week's work here is as good as done. There is just
one bough
On the roped bole, in the fine grey rain,
Green and high
And lonely against the sky.
(Down now! –)
And but for that,
If an old dead rat
Did once, for a moment, unmake the Spring, I might
never have thought of him again.*

*It is not for a moment the Spring is unmade to-day;
These were great trees, it was in them from root to stem:
When the men with the 'Whoops' and the 'Whoas' have
carted the whole of the whispering
loveliness away
Half the Spring, for me, will have gone with them.*

*It is going now, and my heart has been struck with the
hearts of the planes;
Half my life it has beat with these, in the sun, in the
rains,
In the March wind, the May breeze,*

*In the great gales that came over to them across the roofs
from the great seas.
There was only a quiet rain when they were
dying;
They must have heard the sparrows flying,
And the small creeping creatures in the earth where they
were lying
But I, all day, I heard an angel crying:
"Hurt not the trees."*

Laurence Binyon

From: The Burning of the Leaves

Now is the time for the burning of the leaves.
They go to the fire; the nostril pricks with smoke
Wandering slowly into a weeping mist.
Brittle and blotched, ragged and rotten sheaves!
A flame seizes the smouldering ruin and bites
On stubborn stalks that crackle as they resist.

The last hollyhock's fallen tower is dust;
All the spices of June are a bitter reek.
All the extravagant riches spent and mean.
All burns! The reddest rose is a ghost;
Sparks whirl up, to expire in the mist: the wild
Fingers of fire are making corruption clean.

Now is the time for stripping the spirit bare,
Time for the burning of days ended and done,
Idle solace of things that have gone before:
Rootless hope and fruitless desire are there;
Let them go to the fire, with never a look behind.
The world that was ours is a world that is ours no more.

*They will come again, the leaf and the flower, to arise
From squalor of rottenness into the old splendour,
And magical scents to a wondering memory bring;
The same glory, to shine upon different eyes.
Earth cares for her own ruins, naught for ours.
Nothing is certain, only the certain spring.*

WILLIAM H. DAVIES

LEISURE

What is this life if, full of care,
We have no time to stand and stare?

No time to stand beneath the boughs
And stare as long as sheep or cows.

No time to see, when woods we pass,
Where squirrels hide their nuts in grass.

No time to see, in broad daylight,
Streams full of stars, like skies at night.

No time to turn at Beauty's glance,
And watch her feet, how they can dance.

No time to wait till her mouth can
Enrich that smile her eyes began.

A poor life this if, full of care,
We have no time to stand and stare.

WILLIAM H. DAVIES

BORN OF TEARS

A thing that's rich in tears is sweet –
No sounds in all the world are sweeter.
A robin redbreast in the fall,
    The nightingale in June;
The bleating of young lambs in March,
    And the violin in tune:
These are the sounds that haunt my ears,
And all of them are born of tears.

A thing that's rich in tears is fair –
No sights in all the world are fairer.
How lovely is a summer's eve
    That's full of heavenly light;
When tears of joy, called shooting stars,
    Run down the face of night.
While every rainbow that appears
Could say – "My mother's name is Tears."

Edward Thomas

Sedge-warblers

This beauty made me dream there was a time
Long past and irrecoverable, a clime
Where any brook so radiant racing clear
Through buttercup and kingcup bright as brass
But gentle, nourishing the meadow grass
That leans and scurries in the wind, would bear
Another beauty, divine and feminine,
Child to the sun, a nymph whose soul unstained
Could love all day, and never hate or tire,
A lover of mortal or immortal kin.

And yet, rid of this dream, ere I had drained
Its poison, quieted was my desire
So that I only looked into the water,
Clearer than any goddess or man's daughter,
And hearkened while it combed the dark green hair
And shook the millions of the blossoms white
Of water-crowfoot, and curdled to one sheet
The flowers fallen from the chestnuts in the park
Far off. And sedge-warblers, clinging so light

To willow twigs, sang longer than the lark,
Quick, shrill, or grating, a song to match the heat
Of the strong sun, nor less the water's cool,
Gushing through narrows, swirling in the pool.
Their song that lacks all words, all melody,
All sweetness almost, was dearer then to me
Than sweetest voice that sings in tune sweet words.
This was the best of May – the small brown birds
Wisely reiterating endlessly
What no man learnt yet, in or out of school.

THAW

Over the land freckled with snow half-thawed
The speculating rooks at their nests cawed
And saw from elm-tops, delicate as flower of grass,
What we below could not see, Winter pass.

Edward Thomas

There's Nothing Like the Sun

There's nothing like the sun as the year dies,
Kind as it can be, this world being made so,
To stones and men and beasts and birds and flies,
To all things that it touches except snow,
Whether on mountain side or street of town.
The south wall warms me: November has begun,
Yet never shone the sun as fair as now
While the sweet last-left damsons from the bough
With spangles of the morning's storm drop down
Because the starling shakes it, whistling what
Once swallows sang. But I have not forgot
That there is nothing, too, like March's sun,
Like April's, or July's, or June's, or May's,
Or January's, or February's, great days:
August, September, October, and December
Have equal days, all different from November.
No day of any month but I have said –
Or, if I could live long enough, should say –
"There's nothing like the sun that shines to-day."
There's nothing like the sun till we are dead.